Moths

Moths

The illusions you see, they taint this life ...

Illusory Poems #2

CIARAN PERKS

THE CHOIR PRESS

First published in the United Kingdom in 2022 by
The Choir Press

ISBN 978-1-78963-318-4

Contents

Every Head Smaller

Pining and hiding in my disastrous self-reflections
I look towards what I've told myself, the future path!

Destruction, illumination in past regression
to look at my life in the vehicle, I see a sorrowful standing
eighteen plagiarisms in the rear view, and counting every head
smaller
I straddle through the foetal fatal, mirror of children I once
knew
am I destined to follow this infinite drag, infinitely backwards?

I believe I ascend the steps from hell or hell-disguise,
purgatory-masks
but I question why the familiar scents, the asphalt and the
damages
the senses, clouds of ash by dying phoenixes, no head nor tail
to challenge
I am a soul without eyes, hence the blind stalking
back the string path of tireless walking

my death row, counting the years in rewind from the origin
that had me counting
the days I'd follow through confidently confessing
the only obligation I've deemed myself ruling in this travel
but who am I to judge? The same body that parries each
orbital exhaustion
has it breaking the stringent tangents, the memories of desired
and vanished
losing time not from the ageing, but from the hand that has aged.

Ten Years Rewritten

Hardly for me to understand
a didactic fantasy, this transient nostalgia takes me for
a plastic bag in the cyclone
waging fears, tidal yearns, and the pasts make backwash
residing constantly in my acrid airs,
arid of pleasure, humid of sorrows
from the hands of the misunderstood, tiny fists to the wind
will make of these in any lapse of second
moment of damned denial, they will always be
tiny fists wanting these shallow winds dead

foreign are the integrities of change
I am an unforgiving remnant in some already dead mind
but it is to one I have given impact, my rare attempt to remain
memorable
for the lack of attempt at crafting solid legacy
I will never forget the people that reveal
in the lights, the facets of shame, themselves in me
dragging, a divinely detained caricature
keeping himself at home to his unwise motives of penance
the world of nothing can change what has been done
I, then, a fool at playing the doctor to his guilty, declining
conscience

what do I do with my grit? Floored by rehabilitation
is truly debilitating, what must be undone
the provided aches, the settled fakes,
I defame my active agitations, short exchange for the unrequited
that denies me like I deny it
remains easier that way, is what I'd say
if I couldn't admit to the reals in this exhausting kind of decay

I knew somebody, once, desperate for their misguided
salvation
in the short span of a lifetime, and now they are free
from a self-imposed shackle, a personality in tyranny
but that of me could never, trading with the dealer that put me
here
what I'd do to sabotage his inquest of succession,
ten years to be rewritten

devious angst in these spoken agitations that now mean
different
from a lost time's intention
is the story that keeps its mimic, its lisp
the same detriments fond of a story dreadful of repetition
my obsession to be young, to be then
the embodiment of the era not forgotten
but longest gone
a primal feud of me and time, but I know it is it that has won
to dare a constant in its fabrics, I just a seam-split in the sheet
in the ironed-warm understanding of serenities impossible.

Dull Blue Converse Shoes

On this breached eve
once in a full moon's weariness
silent lasting night of the communal hopefulness
there sits in a hollow outlet
the caverned mind overloaded
heavier, the empowered suggestions consult
addiction in misery

shorter the life that is to be led
than is the persuaded soldier, of it, goes halfway dead
stumbling through the obstacle of his own misanthropy
dressed in established rags and
dull blue Converse shoes
Chuck's handmade linen inspires this treading sacrifice
second-hand and the tasteless ventures of the cheap
goes I, stalking in muttered rubber, scars the yellow bricks
blacker than agony
there, so short in a trek too lasted by the realists, the greedy,
sits a ragged pair
an acclaimed marker defines how long it takes
for a healthy boy to become a corpse of his surroundings

it is dark, and like a flagpole they are awaited
white-waving in the ripple-strides of a sighing breeze
as expected, I am scorned by what has displaced me from will
in an instinctual affinity for the average design,
my path is slightly illuminated,
no, stained by the headlights of those that watch me through
backdrop's infamous bushes
like a sadly-sitting deer, pacing for the extremity, the tragedy
clicking heels of worn
the phoney spirit of greetings by the many white beams
shoot through me fuller pits, whole holes
and I am disgraced! I am tired!
Of this surreal floundering

goes through the caterpillar distances
waiting for the chrysalis enchantment
though guilty and without pride, wingless I must stand
in the same dull blue footsteps
that were once expected of me.

Lone Bird Dreaming

Lone bird lusting
away from a breast-pack
uninterested by the popular way of being
enters in the breadth, blurred horizons
of candle-lit skyscrapers and refuge rooms
that birdie flies over

lone bird festers
the sold flights of prior
too hopeful that what has been
will, once again, somewhat be
but there is no greater land
that birdie must cross
than the beaten trenches of impossibility

will nobody give him a hand,
a feather for his wingless drifts?
It is not he, a stationary ball of dream,
that has the whole world to sulk and sift,
it is but the mind of the blondest baby birdie
taken with the transparent doom
of which he sees no cover

dream on, lone bird
and with great spirits becomes great capability
oh, tragedy, hide yourself from our lovely birdie
the one you knew would be too keen for reality
he doesn't yet know
the trivia of a fast-coming disillusionment
too fond of his predictability.

The Emptiest Welcome

This morning was of hardship
I couldn't muster the want to
escape that land of myth and fiction
but for the fake world pretending of real
so must I
on the left, stack of serene and high
where to rest my head, this bed-side that convicts
has at me no mercy in its doom gestures
foreshadowing the muds I call instinct

I watch out, over too far away
too long the distance that I care enough to make
but my eyes have lied to me
and it is these dark lids that have me wake
I am a boy of disingenuous introversion
soul-full of him, and that enigma I can't decompose
its funny sense of making me wish
the ways weren't of such cruel nature
or because of the seclusion that gets bold
overstays the emptiest welcome
I have become, over the wasted hours, immature

if I can't have it real, I'll have it mine
whether the stupid or the irritable,
or the distinction of decline
the optimist, here, now cries
a leisure in the ceremonial hopelessness
I can't discern whether I revel in its company
or prevail in the perils of its dictatorial mastery
I know we all have our own versions of toil
as mine have been extrapolated and spoiled
from the hole that I leave to the hole that has me grieved
I am ignorant in that storage pleasure,
then I bring with me the radiances, the echoes of the believed
to permanently rest with the definites.

With What He's Tried

With what I've tried
and there, flaw in the thousands
fleeting like a rag in the winds
perched in some subway, some underpass revelation
begging for the fabrics of wealth
deemed allergic on him

he has lost his affinities,
his tastes are as forgotten as famine
for the life of a good man
it is not possible, mileage remains
one sorrowful litre of consolation
I beseech the one that holds me
like a mother never could
I beseech the one that listens
like a snake never would

he is, in recent days, quieting
bringing on the silences
that are as equal as violence in the mind
a victory with the motive to kill
or find him fallen off the torn chair
holding this spilling bottle of wet weaknesses
like a boulder in the eye and standing gracefully
and the pin bends like spineless
the boulder is sewn to shake and shiver
murdering the pin with its load

his eyes have contained
those same weights of genuine torment
he lays sleepless, or limps through the obligation
and with what I've tried,
he falls from stable to imperfection.

Mellow Pleasures

Uncultured by a tumultuous decree
moments unlearning the habit
of days spent in with the company of another
as if detachment had the ability to determine
what it is those go without greater thought
than the last seconds going gone

whispers on the isle, section I lay
like a plank of wood, of use if used, if could
the hours of the day, my friends that play
around this slat of splinters solely misunderstood
the toes that make ballet and have tipped themselves high
the waitresses of the untouched roads
hitchhikers of the legs and pacing, holding bags filled of
advertisement
and swinging in the breeze, more important the new uniforms
than greenery or grocery
temporary and quickly stale, this unreal attraction

they drift, they die in the scenes
coolly perched as some to lay with me,
too loud of ascertained claims to make observation
too stuffed of thought, pillow-head sensation
too vague to get the truth in grey ideas
matterless hue that skips occasionally
this moment in yellow treasure, gratefully
mellow pleasures, fortunately

the sun is ripe on this virgin afternoon
may the whispers pass like rumours fade,
like lie's last waltz in the street-plead
the sun has made my dim eyes bleed.

To Me, Wherever I Have Gone

I am a pinstriped child dressed with a rubber ring
in the shallow pools of human
a matchless identity of his own substanceless mind
seemingly lost in the deeper ends never paddled

artificially, I put my personas to the edge of fruition
they only know the jester, the character of a fraudulent
authenticity
I couldn't stress more value of truth in these words
my actor, my glory, hidden in the maze tongue of black-on-
white
though as monochromatic my self pity formulates,
the rainbows are truly transparent, people have mistook the
colours of my charisma with solidarity

I am a comparison that I have made
that is fond of the nonexistent orgasm of clarity
there is vagueness in this misunderstanding of me
there is not enough in life's duration to demonstrate
that of which I really am
the facade is a better slope slipped
and sliding I trip
clumsy on the contemporary comedies of my caricature

I am a shadow of the character, possession in this self
the four walls of my claims, they are a parody
they laugh at me, in the scorn that I have provided
so funny more, to laugh at what he pretends to understand

I am a catalogue of likes and dislikes,
but by which company am I being sold?
I have sold myself the shortness of inclination
that of which I am devoid; a fish in the tank he doesn't
recognise
one to be born, the same of its grave
the glass bowl Earth with muds and mires, dreads and desires
irretrievably distant to me of any moment that is pinned

on the event horizon to a black hole of consciousness
to who has this hold has it on a person,
I couldn't say it was me.

Resident Irrelevance

In this familiar room,
this familiar gloom,
stained olive and washed with blueberries
weirdest colour of these halls
this man sits
as if he was young

old friends in the flats of time
which does he look through?
Nine, and sees them laughing in infancy
fourteen, and sees the snows soon scream
seventeen, comes into contact, prior recollection
that makes nineteen fearful of the locked door

it's a quiet room, next to his
the boy that pretends and the boy that suspends
his thoughts like irony in a room of shame
his words like excuse to the airs lame
sometimes there is knocking, but never has the door unlocked
a latch that must budge, like a trigger that soon must cock

the curtains are pulled over, no cheating
time doesn't allow insight
back to my room,
resident irrelevance, this man.

Bedtime for the Skeleton

Bedtime for the skeleton
in his blankets of flesh
weighing down the apparition of the wrist
or the fascination of stomachs hollow
makes a grave-indentation in the mud mattress
that he'll permanently follow

bedtime for the skeleton
who once could not be seen
more than what room absorbed
the essence of over-welcome and too keen
when his wrists start carving, when the ribs contort
starving is the trick of a fatty's retort
and it is his last resort

bedtime for the skeleton
who takes to an activity dull
woefully soured and wasting
his mind is the only part of him to remain full
drought of health, the sleepy outline of a boy knows
you cannot vomit your thoughts, in filthy vain
crucified by troubles that slowly turn skin to bone.

New Cobbles for Permanence

Permanent skies are rolling in on
my greener sides of rather be
I have killed my enthusiasm perfectly
each attempt at giving into the blue way of doing things

bricks never been more red
never been more stained with the silence
nor the hustle of thoughtful regret
though just once, as far as it'll reach
I have finally become enthused to forget

I graffiti my memories in a cosmic black
to halt the glow of memories rush back
into the forefront of a future's damned demise
the time of a lesson to learn is one I despise

no clouds, no hanging white spreadsheet in the rainy logistics
not a splash of ink to oblige or obey
as incredulous it may sound, as sadistic
I rid myself an opportune freedom for one more day

there is no liberty in restriction of thought
as much as I pretend this to be a lesson taught
if I revel in the disparaged comfort of solitude
as the sun, a centre of isolation's warmest magnitude
to a degree at which is incomprehensible
I remain predictable

settling in the permanence, I can speak a calm rarity
wash me understood in the spring airs
I tread new cobbles carefully.

Current Ways

What ever made me think
it was the right time to be understood?
Not even when I like my circumstance
and I can ruin a good moment
like bad taste in worse company
I only needed what I thought was gone
then how can I feel a slab under my feet
and not the warm covers of my sheets?

There are at least a few
or, I don't know, a very special specific
in the realms of people
that I contemplate the wrongdoing of past's failure
whether action, fading, or emotion
and all three apply to the situation
of current ways.

Sapling Damned

My soul is swelling
with a paranoid dread on your arrival
longing couldn't even compare
to this hole of resentment
I didn't even think about the reaction
a shy boy could give, timidly,
to the one who made him wait

what you do not know is
I've lived only to have lost
I am not afraid to die for the one who reveals
the hands I've clobbered to hold
behind a back that has been turned
I'd never use it as my target, though
it is the same of these eyes to have burned, then
drenched

I cry for someone I do not now know
I yearn for someone I could never have
I don't know who I was
yet he was the one who had you
I've been condemned to the prison of pining
your image across, the best scarring of my mind
and for that, how could I repay you?

Messy as hidden murder, the scene in my sheets,
my ruffled quilts agitated, my wet pillow head
weary of the dampened silk lining over tired lids
plugging the fleeting, feeling, reeling
kneeling on the promise of a predator that prays
and I know, for this I am only the most certain, I am no god
so why does it prey on me?

I live and I suck the airs of arid pressure
contentment in this passive beating
that calendars have made punch bags of my waking
while the stars make folk-love from my nightmares
tell it in the constellations
make my head Jerusalem, my heart Bethlehem
take the hay from my scattered manger mind
and be born again under the ever-present stain
that we stand between the longest distance
of those lost years

and what do we have to say for them?
As we did, as boys but now only
man to boy, I am a sapling
and your jungle sag is wallowing
beneath the wax fibrous rays
candle-lit bravado through a sunny facade
buttress-breadth and betting on
the next day I fall victim to the reddest soils
so do it again, make me bleed, in deadest toils
I cope again with your next goodbye, the hand that pleads
so good it shall be, so good it is I hope.

In My Dated Mind

I have to see other people
I hate it
to be forced away from that line of thought
always directing towards the same image

what am I to do
as the blue always seems tender for black?
How am I supposed to go about
forgetting, not looking back? My eyes are
rear-view mirrors, they lie
the object it thinks is closer
is so many years beyond
the distances of empty

first, or only
but never what it should have been
I speak in the vague tongue
they hunt my clarity like diamonds
little do they search the sack of sorrow
for its enchantments
and sparingly leave me
as if these diamonds are balloons
bag of lighter than air
is what I know to be hollow bag
nowhere for empties to die

transient nothingness
make these wishes springtime
because I've missed a few blooms
or soon, a parody of these wishes floating
merry-go-animals, slaves to the child's underside
rocking back and even further behind the doom
of eyes too wide
how old do you think I am? I have
the sense of nobody older than nine
and the innocence of a positive pregnancy test

when the womb kicks you out
to make you pay its host rent
the flames of world on milk toes

heavenly, angel-sent
the graveyard march beats its percussion
every of my birthdays
like the dry horse I'm knackered
for the puppies of hardship

the vehicle for stressing
takes to grind its wheeled soles
forward the days of fuel-capped
wearing the laces, the toddler torso,
the blondest car on the motorway
breaking down next to a crematorium
not even roadkill will trade this worry
for road-life

thankfully I'm just a passenger to
an idiot's samey devices
it is what happens
when the driver expects to be driven
by the paralysed.

Ivory Bindings

I resent it
these loins, this body of being, is it, only good
young and curious?
I know it is still young
so baby-like, no shred of guilt
perfectly hidden behind the rare smile
no angst or ounce of distaste
in my once more pleasant words,
ones typically spoken
like dreaded rains in the summer
they fog up the lens of my humid awkwardness
over the contemplation
over unrequited distraught

new love, I could never practise
because it isn't going to be as perfect as
old hatred for the dead companionship
I'd rather its killer
come and knock on my willing door
how the door will react
open-hinged and ready to give warmest hospitality
to the one who leaves his knife carefully placed
through my back

bitterly, I avoid it
the sight, the scent, the scene of you
we have common ground
shared by long distance
we have mutual understanding
your escapade now, and she is
revolting
your husky brunette charlatan
that clings to your arms like leprosy
the spastic thong on fishnets
and she keeps making it clearer
as if your misty mirrors were too difficult to discern
misty on me, as I have missed you?

I doubt you'll ever
bring yourself to change your mind
it is guaranteed, while not an impossibility
to be as rare as guiltless atrocity
I have small, outstretched fingers
crayons digging the parchment grave
of my tearful features
they decorate me so immature
they turn me lax to wax
and melt like the heart of her
when your perfect love has strangled it
like my constricted yearns
sulking like cheeks burning
I am skinned, my asphyxiated loving
plays dead on the letter
I am fused to the stamped agony
of my words that will never meet you.

Dream-Child Dress-Up

Sentimental dream-child
I grip strongly
to the dying fragments
my memories lay in the hospital mind
on ward six, yes,
cancer ward for dreams of
cancer, cancer, cancer
some vomit in buckets, drunk on hope
others transfuse their love, to be clean
of the worst plague of the body
the weakness of disposition

the doctor has this cancer
and he is not qualified
he's just dressed up in the white coat
because the cold truth that runs thick
in these permanently isolated walls
he knows it doesn't get better
died twice in the acceptance
we are liberated in our freezing desires
and I will lay down with all of you,
each head with the nose pipe
each arm with the crack pipe
each mouth with the persuasion
so eat it up, swallow every pill of irony
that may be the death of you
I know better, in my white coat

dream-child dress-up
let's play it out
where is the visitor? Oh
he visits at least ten of them
a bouquet for longing
a petal for dread
in leafy vain, he gives me the soil
that plots my grave.

Fool Talks and Tires

Blue day today,
I know that because I had opened the curtains to see it
that familiar look, the reflection scares me wholly
and I made haste to retreat to the haunting
the activity is hazy, the salt lines are crossed, dared by
emptiest traded body for a red coward
dull, fat, and timeless his physique of getting-there
I am consistent in these heats to struggle in

cracked vase
you can hold love in your hole for a week and a half
then the sweetest words fall frail on the failures
of your incompatible brim
I knew a love like cracked vase
the thorns reside, the contraction at the bottom and scathingly
rots the way its honeymoon promises fell guilty
red is your victim, shadows that you photosynthesise

low spirits, so the percentage is great for me
I return back to the one watching on that tainted shelf
at least he is available to return to
I wish I was a bottle of tequila
so the one who used to seek his battered solace
could share the secret of me in the warmest lips
of a tightly-breasted mare

it is inevitable, we should lie together again
years of truth withheld
years of parody, of parade
I have to laugh! If not, the silence becomes hanging
like the transcending of suicide
and it is lovely to know
the next time we lie together
is in a bed of mud.

Stale Binary

My love is like stale bread
buttered to the core but drying
served to the gods, it's the best I could do
bread rising, I have been called
and risen from the crumb trash
my love is binned

dreamless evenings call endless nights
I wake with the aggravation of knowing
that is the eternity I stay
to wake from it is just the insult I need
I lay awake like a cheating maid
I wish to be sent there, once more,
like an unread love letter

how much longer, than already it has been long,
to think of this? I am the expert,
I have spent too long
refining the craft of sour taste
I bet I am better than mourners
longing for selfish convincing
I know my capacity for grief
poisons pleasure, stains comfort

there is never a dull moment now,
not when each moment takes
to forget, or to remember
the wicked binary I have come to adorn
in my plated regrets
it builds me like rusty armour
the tears that oxidise these coldest innards.

Brim on Brink

The circumstance was midnight
or just about nearing
I was dressed in the same shanty style
four or five days in
I convinced them all I was changed
each morning with a new grin

just by my life, my business there sits
a three-metre deep overcast
shroud of rushing water
I walk by the bed, the banks of bleached grass
sponge of the summer I tread
for footsteps that rarely make themselves known

deceiving those the actual common path
was a path never travelled
we've all walked some sort of path
if we think there is a path to walk

enough of it, I say brim on brink
red in cheek, head above head
sitting once more near the hills rolling
time is now gone, there is no keeping it serious
in the place that's thought no more of me
than a joke! And that's what it is
the very

that gives me pleasure,
like the breeze rippling over
that wet maze of my plunge
may this skin that dampens downstream
be that to give you the very same chill.

Great British Dissonance

I knew it when I did
the old telling of face
wrong; though I couldn't

tell me, then, the face I believed
to be different,
am I right to say
it was just growing?

Unfamiliar to me
and my faulty remarks.

I ask this for he who sees through
fumbling by like three years
on the dusk of penance
may midnight be longer
for he who refuses it.

Like this, I put the curse
on when I dare await another
recollection is the murder of the self
and longing is the brandished knife
committing

I mistake myself for a butcher
those abattoir years.

Decade's Driest Choke

My youngers I mourn
blessed they to have dared become
what it is that talks in his shroud
years long in grief
the deadliest inebriation
you've corked eternally my head
drinking from your bottle cap kisses

you trapped me a webbed disaster
within the spun calamities of your silk image
we have Stockholm love
I am reborn every morning of what it does to me in solitude
the weak phoenix with the luck of a swine
as one-sided as the cards you keep to the chest
as subsided, any remnant or chance of valentine

I remember it like obligation
stacked hours triumphant in brazen presence
what beautiful fantasies, what miserable dreams!
In three murders, you wounded some years of me
the spirit hanging like teenagers
immature on my delicate person

I will cease in this, blue boy's
crippled mind
as a carrot does in the broth of its
selfish peers' wills of plugged
transfusion may your tongue be that I speak on
the language of a man that hides

many there were, the scripted evenings we acted on
no heart-strings attached
call me the puppet
his cotton life, stuffings all over the mattress
you ate me like Christmas day
my wings are insults to me
when it is this cage you've preserved yourself through
the iron of my flightless visage
now in the gold-most browns of debris

rusty, metal paradise facade
a cool husk I've become
the soulless exhaustion that warms only by
the touch of a good memory gone bad
I have that dire effect; cherishing falls on me
like a morgue's excreted enterprise
into the mud clots,
ten toes on the long-dead pleasures of me
frost-bitten in the angst of lost time
cherishing is mutilated, stands only resentment

I look at you through
the lunchtime of our lives
you have my gaze from across our benched distance.
If you happen to go without legacy
forever, then, remembered only in my past eyes

decade's driest choke
it can only be told in the lip that quivers
never again a real smile glides
on my pageant-ready masquerade
mouth of would-have sighs

is this the amounted, our strong connection
as hopeless as blocked numbers,
I get to speak of the irretrievable serenity?

We as parted is what unites us,
what we as partnered divides.

For April's Rendition

Black lines benign thoughts
white traces it, the copy-cat colour
in great distaste of its hopeful purposelessness
the sly wit of a cotton grey conundrum
amounting to the distressing debris
that lost minds hesitate to accept

sky lighting up like June, when it is
another of April's turns
deceiving, raging like political demeanour
in the executioner's spare bedroom
where he'd keep his second-hand jewels and swoon
over the lamp-lit beheading of his summer girl's
last taste of blue, gripping on the final afternoon
shady ways, blurring days in the wet-eyed gloom

bleak undermines the warming opportunity
and spite chases it, the emotion of recurrence
astonishing, the isolation from the sentient streets
begging with the knee-hungry in the method of grey
strikes like penalty, the penultimate trial to the rain
lasting seemingly eternal,
clouding over obscurity, wool-scabbards for teary blades

white void over the black heart
oil sleeves over milk arms
my petty opulence, a fraudulent disdain
wrapped over with manger-intent to pretend
there is worth in an empty pocket
drown in kings' old and good remarks
for what they believed to be right, what I tend to defy
appoint me greatly predicted, I reflect disappointment
coolly glides on sentiments, this winter afflicted
what looming yearn, disillusionment has me addicted
on the same lesson, I never learn.

Baby Boy from Ciretose

Throat stops
in the heats of being breathless nineteen
the shrinking vessel collapse

my bones of stardust shredding
my melody of misery compelling
compulsions of mannerism in the way of mindlessness
that deity, that figure of monkey's destined path
streets of peel, my yellow bricks to fall over
skin ripe like plump apricot
but whiter than spoilt milk
children's sheets, ironed like designer
the linen-blood foolishness that shapes me

needn't control is how this acts
the silhouette that ruins
the silhouette, black dream with two legs that runs further
than its dimensional counterpart was willing
I am the shadow to what the shadow should be of me
a truth behind figment that crawls through
and through, spider or toddler
learning movement is ironic
in still living,
change is the charmless tale of others
it was my turn, as evidently wrong as unforgiving

old potential was a danger
slipping with his adamant carer
pair of irrelevance, drastic pestilence grips me endlessly
the boring revelation, I ceaselessly invite
the manners of a misanthrope
awkwardly shunning those that I deter
it makes me poor, seeing the gallery stacks
altering motives in the plastic neons of total containment
advancement of the troglodyte
with primitive pink shoes and cyan eyeshadow
dresses the whores of antibiotics and apnoea
by pleasure's ego dump, these celebrated rites
rituals for those that claim desired
as if it were really true, old potential now new loss

like shopfront ivy, like superstore moss
dust on the unaffordable,
a health of debris in charismas retired.

Moths

So many, so many
dizzy and drowsy in the lands lost and plentiful
in the distance, from a bus stop
a bedroom light is lit, a mouse-hole in a maze street
I couldn't be sure, I felt I knew his determination
an old friend clawing at his rigidity,
the expensive lilac wallpaper of his sanity
now reveals magnolia boredom in bad standard
this town likewise, bricklaying the fever in the insulation
they choke on family spirit
they and this slate-soul situation
the crowds, taking shape of chimneys and oak hinges
reclusive charcoal patterns, the obituary flame that tinges
warmth in the common familiarity
people inflicting their dull farmyard scratches
counting the days on the finest lines of wire
weird chickens without authority.

The uglies of this frequency
giving great evidence, petty suffering
insubordinate refugees to the golden prosperous lie
are the electric-bill angels, splendour of dark rooms
cheap glooms, dampened dooms
the light of guidance shunned by a rainy day
wings cut by tax-man's guilty hand
sheep in a one-eyed cloth, made cavern gargoyles
from the marbles of their crumbling pedestals
he who finds warmth in the blanket of torn wallpaper,
she who spends her living wage on the necessary summer
accessory

genetically disbanded in the grievances
desperate leather wallets of allotted promise
one day, a day that slowly drags
its battered feet on the paved calendar slabs of mortality
its needy knees, as worn as grabbing hands, praying hands,
Russell's bulimic boxers to the punch bags of warping image
instils the expected fear in a jaded castaway inspired,
as they do the graveyard shrines of Mary succumbing.

Like moths, they must swarm
like bleak thoughts in cocoon's sheltered isolation
the caterpillar offspring of sickle-breast indication
blessed pale, enriched the present gift a revelation
what is left from the horse-racing goes only the bloody systems
punished bodies of work, mound-minds pulled by trash
consolations
half-living, the other without a reason to be fought for
like the blank mercy held in every child's unwilling hand
the same for every beating bullet shot from the cocked tin-
cup of hungry men
soldiers are the starved puppies of greed's luckiest ninth life
soldier, the six-pack practitioner of the prideful shanty house,
or soldier, disciple of the cheese, a red-faced mouse?
Money as tight as her stockings,
his throat rotting from the raw consumption of unfiltered breaths,
blonde wisteria dresses my saddened lenses,
prettiest fuchsia stained by trench-mud,
under a pink sea, over a white-flag sky
like moths, they must fly.

Same Circles Spun

Back the strongest swallow
in the thin-throat life, guilt takes the immune form of pride
give out your hand, worm fingers on hook intention
perhaps I'll be persuaded
as tamed, training the legs of a paraplegic
ill, in the slowest attempt of recovery
the medics come prodding, love as sharp as scalpels
kindness in the colloquial hiss-tongue
predator-trust in my playground-world purgatory
rushed compulsions of sulks
not uncommon of injury

it matters no more
wondering the wrongdoings, no surprise in agony
no persistence in good lacking
there is peace in the hardly walked streets
muddy canyons of mulled green and marsh
beaten by sole spades
leaning on the undead transgressions
benches dot poppy views, for the stupid waiters
expecting the rain to cry gold
and hands to come shake the misery
straight up from the burial

a better day is hard of complaint
but there always manages it, the fastened continuity
permanently through pompous ripples of aching time
seems to rant, a spat-and-silly tyranny

there is now peace in the palanquin
humble-most rooftop and warm curtains soothe labour days
from saddened shoulders to cloud-high legs,
upping out a grave-sodded Earth
from its toil-root truths to its numbness
as secret as plaster on true world's touch
makes you bleed whether or not you are ready for it
beneath the scorching wisdoms
clods of battered mutiny lace the mires of a thinking man's skin
rests the scalped pellets of an impure milk

bland expression from my making
blandest sat on the cakes and the candles
there is boredom in the wishes blown out of proportion's
birthdays
tiresome is greedy obligation, loneliness forces this condition
you can view me in the picture show of my memories
if ever they are replayed in physicality
but if I go by the time the printers waste these unnecessary inks
I'll be shown through rumour, daren't the willingness says
evil in my bleak method
skimming your short time over my relentless rejection
I have learnt this only from the days I have seen

this is the realm of humanity
consistent, perfect in its faults
cog empire of embryo failures
the same circles spun of this malignant clockwork
turns thoroughly over all of which I dwell.

In Fog

World for people wrong world for me
endless landscape, the injustice of my experience
faintly sleeps under a sour horizon
reduces the corner of an eye to a bad sight
wilting wet petals beneath a crescent eternity
ongoing way with the shaded hindrance
the echo of this prejudice burns my cold emotion
into a wax puddle that awaits new ignition
with only wicked soul

crave sleep
the longest linen dresses empty dreams
infant carcass compared to
the forevers I fixate
unpredictable bodies, to think some would interact
a biased prediction foretells only failure
feared assumption inspires imperfect fruition
the faultless dares of desire
whether wished upon or woefully occupied

in bones, bloods,
messes the transience of ordered awareness
a black room is the closest I'll get
closed eyes touching me better
intercourse of physicality and mortality
fondled by the blind lingerie then torn from
my fibrous connections are rigid but not invincible
woven by inherited threads I strip with pride
like a foolish full moon
in fog.

Hecklers' Treasures

Relapse of the body submission of the mind
this bitter pettiness, method of constriction,
must this be the way my better days are spent?
I agree to enrichment with hesitance
undeserving of the fruitful condition
I have already killed the wills, the values, and vows
dense like cattle grounds for the hog feud
different pleasures for different measures
mine are in the aggravated kilo
nineteen degrees to lowly

I give it thought
wrongful turns, think about it
descended my young pillar like an infantile Zeus
finding the thunder clouds now limp of saturation
sorry gusts of damp debris, grey bags for a face's flaccid distress
willing to offer my body so easy, rejection then identifies
what I've bothered to conduct of worthlessness

milk sheets porous of connection
bring heavy dread beyond the cobalt confidences
that bludgeon my look between the same gaze
strained uglier each moment of exchange
the towel baby, hope in its once attractive smiles
disgust can barely make it a smirk now
towel baby, proud nurses that congregated beyond
maternity's hungry grip
grows like a slug but for the drudgery
prowls like a slut but for solitude
howls like wimp-paws but for slumber

forever wanders a slow child
treads silently on the outskirts of everything
timid head begs for the home
millions of miles away in memory
naive heart begs for hecklers' treasures.

Losses in Blackout

My empathy,
like a skinny blonde with cracked glasses
once standing half a man
crying no more in pillows
but in the arms that do not hold him
goes home to harsh regard and hapless torment
they all then come to ask
why did he do it?

My passion
like a cabin in Californian woodland
houses a solemn robin on its decks
a solitary squatter in its bathroom
so easily turned into the charred stardust
like every other thing lost in the past
they all then come to ask
why do they go?

My charm
like a stable family home
with a stable family love
the brotherless son sleeps in
possession play-pits, friendless dreams
where he sneaks into the first floor
of real family love
just to have it dismantled
they all then come to ask
what was the reason?

I have narrators
for the empty of my page
scrapbook ghostwritten
to be told by the lying lips
of those who pretend to be loved ones.

Secrets from the Abandonment

There is still one who loves you,
little boy,
he resides as does the guiltless hope
drowns in what never comes
I put my hand in yours
we walk together emotionless
blue stadium that laughs with
the inevitably ill hysteria,
to endorse confinement
is confessional acceptance for rude punishment

conditioned to imitate the standard of the idiot
gatekeeping righteousness to frigid models
or figures who dare steal that fortified role
gleam of the successor's blind eyes
without notice we crossed each other's
miserably low valley paths
stress level mightier than Babel
as mythical to those on the other side
of the indulgent magnifying glass,
safety behind the critically impactful opinion

criticism comes bold in a list of insufferable actions
when knowing the pivotal pretension
is as difficult to answer as absurd theory
gets you clawing at the cradle-cap edges
the scalped artichoke decomposes
and the tender morals unfurl
under the oxidised iron veil
burning warmer than love's propaganda,
the one who has the power to touch you
then touches another;
it is this kind of hollow.

There is still one who loves you,
little boy,
and other secrets I share with the mirror.

Compression Impressions

Sleep, or relaxation, or comfort,
I need to take my turn of a break
I need a breather, I haven't the lungs
I face the discouragement of the following day
angst in this intolerance
weak hands that endlessly turn my hardship
into messy black ink pools
on paper's fractured edge.

Frustrations Mortally

Strangers become lovers in the room I rot
in a teary corner
sobbing incoherent confessions to the flies
that buzz carelessly between thoughts and intentions
it seems paper is my rival, challenging
tormenting more spineless etching as abrasive
shredding white beauty in black bereavements
diaries that coax me into spilling embarrassments
I become the remarks they made of me
I perfect the misdiagnosed superstitions
I bring the best truth from defamation.

Cowardice in Cold Contortion

Refugee sets the rendezvous
two thirds of a half-life
the only brims touched
hourglass violently thin of sand aggravation
its own sigh could bring out a tired wind
into hurricane exhaustion

the boldest diaphragm at work like
satin vomit of eight-leg's injustices
knitting between the femur forceps
struggles fruition in bed-bug retirement
retreat of haired inconsistency
bargained by the webbed fates
it continues to weave

there is idiocy in memory
there is emergency in its dying crime
three toils troubled and trembling
through the tireless tragedy of ticking time
musters the plot for a zombie
roaming its revered remnants on damp countrysides
the cubicle crop efforts as subdued as an office summer
or as suppressed as bad lust's awful taste
in the cheating, unkind of escapism

stuck is the happened hazardous
happening again on pattern's common spread
mistreated the butters of famine
feared as rats waltzing to flute flu,
nettle-rings, continued commitments of unforgiving dread
a debt that lingers long after living
is somehow paid in beneficiary's charitable respects
spoiled retorts of the ignorant
some hill that suffers stone legacies of defiled courage

cruel comforts of cowardice in cold contortion
greater than succession in monetary confinement
wealth in solitary securities
begs the differed drifter
overstaying the unwelcoming, the unbecoming
myths in bone-tights
sought wishes starved of granting.

Today's Guilty Closure

Sombre merriments brush over
the desolate, unchanged roads
in their leisurely forms of distant retirements
seemingly foolish to think about now
there is no guarantee they breach my presence
years away ages my mind
cellar thoughts for the barrel man
vineyard transience for soul-wine
I could still endure this floating
rolling cloud, rainy-day living
whether a sip or a bottle into
the inescapable forecast

I've damaged you,
fine body, enough
more than what I could discern of its worth
baby has me on the edge of his haggard hands
bruised blemishes of brilliance
recognised like gold in rough ambiguity
had awaited times become karats of gleeful disregard
like grudges of those who feign solaces
lies the peace in dated love
relics sent from the naivety
reminders of undisclosed old ways

an era of tranquillity
chance to hardly think, weightless by denial
to confront the ongoing intimidation
gridlocked by unfortunate calendar expectancies
sharpened significantly as refined proclamations
disagreeing character of individuality
it is independence that is criticised
in what is supposed to be tomorrow's news
drained of bitter sediments
pained of intensely fading sentiments
as business-casual sees ripened days
rots the energy of overthinking in casualty.

Shortest Unbecomings

I see the hourly same
eyes dried by repetitive sights
surprise is a mundane feat
another memory to die as I will

born to be the appropriate album
fitting for a bookshelf
bookmarked by eras bookended
by unfortunately tapering
interest subtly declining into a creased page
books read by the scar of its intended leave-off
left off on bookshelf's appropriate desertion

I become a leaflet details the shamble tenure
permanence was a desire too greedy
limitation's incredible abuse on opportunity
unfurling like the gift of learning
disaster stricken when least ready
ribbons that strangle me by realisation
dying a small guide of disappointment
though I became the best a student could be
in a lifestyle uninformed

send me a good love
like a son on the war train
certain to do good.

Eternity's Babel Rest

On the top of a
world for others
those who have placed this blue burden
on the shoulders of their children
nothing as beautiful to unload
disgrace on
those who have torn out their void sections
and made plague on purity

whatever comes to occur
new fixations in later dates
later fortunes, latest findings
wise are those who share life's misinformation
good are those who ignore it
whether lazy or unbothered
detriment at the lowest effect
brilliantly strives on painlessness
never a mistake to be made
never a new lesson then learned

disparaged by
the mightiest constant of an end
it does not exist, the renowned fear
we have named it atrocious
we have blamed the biggest nothing for our faults
just to make clear of stressed consciousness
as endless sleep, we do not recognise, will offer

my next love interest
no person could give this certain immense satisfaction
than a limitless pleasure
it would either take supernatural lips to kiss
or stripped of the tools to dare such a thought
as one of these options expresses their whereabouts
it is when that I fret to acknowledge
most call it destruction
I call it misunderstanding
eternity's Babel rest
unconcerned, at best.

His Ideal Hotel

I knew somebody
who wanted to run a good business
home-holder for luxury
nighttime provider industry
fine linens just to dry oneself
thin panes of glorious hospitality
inscribe the model-facade's five stars
five temporary turns on the tarmac

his estranged philosophies
needn't the brightest advertisement
nor the biggest newspaper spot
it would be that if the people wanted great option
it would be a fateful finding, fortune's fragility
it would be something of this nature

as though a held heart beats in the right mind
I assumed too quickly that
you could not call a place wholesome
once conditioned, the fools with the figments.

His hotel did better than what I could have dreamed
my degradations as typical taste in a spoiled tongue
finally acknowledged in a far mind gone close
I have been dissuaded from destructive doubt
and it feels unsafe.

What are you supposed to do?
Unrighteous belief prevails like snow winds in
apocalypse;
what are you supposed to do
when rain becomes of seemingly permanent ice,
when the clouds make light of the darkest days,
when constant truth makes liar of you?

Whatever happened to the inclinations of the rough?
It was more to me than just his ideal hotel
it was more just to be wrong.

Wings of Ribs

I met common decency
in the form of her red hair
and the poetic way
she dressed framed pictures
of perfectly placed tuesday afternoons
throughout shelves of plastic ivy and persistence

there was intended method
as offhandedly stylistic in the dismissal
as true sense was made in
the compositions of her,
found in when she trained her flytraps
to eat something other than the fly,
she wouldn't want to hurt anything.
The images of her,
found in coffee scrawls and shadow plots,
notebooks of dainty inks
as galleries should endorse

I endorse this kindness
original as sin happened upon me
I am engrossed in otherwise fictitious,
something as innocently brilliant,
someone as impossibly and consistently
a supplement of gracious spirits.

I must've forced something when it was tried
puzzled to find our features couldn't fit,
the fact I don't hear of her reassurances anymore
shows there is no coexistence of perfection and near-enough;
if that is how highly I think of myself,
anything close to her standard as flight to a bird,
then I am misled.

Bitter Lengths

Fluorescent petal tears,
its willow head-resting,
the crown,
it ruled, did you
happen to find
the loving-not nation?

Throne, perched in steel garments;
croaking toad of squelch movement,
the coaxed dissatisfaction.
Lettuce hypothalamus,
melting on a
single buttercup brow.

Hopeless Search for a Hapless Past

Our bond was created from the simple reason
that I wouldn't have needed to pay for something that was free
so I let you fly your jets over
my screwed unit, the landing strip body
a fern-dotted settlement among the bees
hives flooding branches bark next to dog-flea
and flee I would rather away from this obligation
I feel contained, held back, my senses of uncertainty
if your price was on some listed desire
may you have found another, I am the liar
my inscription is resolute, my tapestry foresees
the immature subscription of your naivety
held up, the pillar of distraction
and a pedestal of my image is low
but you find it is one of mild attraction
I was told, this duality would be the richest experience
in this part of my time, my wealth has met a heavy decline.

Take what you can get, this is what I've always said
and yet I find it is difficult to take my own advice
on the precipice of suggestion I couldn't climb
and half of the way, it cannot suffice
second-most and second-best
the compromises degrade me, it forces me less
falling like kittens too curious for their height
and tremble nine fictions on the story of fright,
the brevity of this game I knew
I cut like the corner street from crowded curlicue
weaving my cobble rivers and oxbow-scar crescents

ageing with erstwhile footsteps makes up my presence
if I was heaven my gates would be locked and electrocuted
never opened, rusted, trespassers will be prosecuted.

My open arm atrocities are a contrast
they take applications, they will reject
if you aren't of a standard to be scrutinised,
you are significant enough only to be of neglect
I manage this toil
this instruction,
this cartilage, torn ligament
from the hand of destruction,
sipping from a chalice of bloody oil, fables dress the brim
daren't you turn these tables, on ice you'll run thin.

Houses look the same on this road of unknown fame
chimney smoking like our lungs
a punishment sounds better when the substance is wetter
coming from the licks and the lust of a leper's tongue
but numb are these flames raging in my walls
of obsolete priors
I'll stay to inhale the smog, the fumes
of my self-started dooms and fires
and caged in my walls I'm the pet to my hatred
I'll screech like the bird
flying from one dark corner of a room
to the other damp side of mildew
I'll rot in this tomb, a threat I've heard.

The fences are soggy with their posts clear grey
the paint cuts away like light rays behind clouds
the atmosphere is like my aura, it's in vain
the vision is foggy and lays in the blanket shrouds
but comfort is gone like lithium minds
you have one, it is available, it is soft, it is weak
smooth feelings, when you've seen truths, they're unforgiving
signs
and you have to take your cover when an end is what you seek
I am aware of my unfashionable disguise to this place
I dress in a skin tired and lax
there is only one reason as to why I resent my new face
youth is something I refuse to give back.

Hydrangea Lies

Hydrangea lies
hydrangea drowning
pink and fluttered
with her pursed blush
on beneath a slick chlorophyll band
hesitant of bursting with the lustrous contemplation
opening her jaw reveals thistles,
this hydrangea, the snake's only true rose?

May Mrs. Rosey get on by,
floral in spring
awaiting her summer high
nary a day she wasn't ready
weary her stay beseeched soil rifling
rumbles flesh,
the palm flat and cooling
she didn't care,
she didn't even think about
the other flowers,
her dying stare
stricken by the bee
a nectar despair,
pollinated strain
putting one, bull-red in her brain,
the ground tests Mrs. Rosey
two petals death-tied,
hydrangea lies.

A Tragedy in Black

Despair has its unkind taint
fluent in the uncountable hour
distinct in memorable quality
short joy in large quantity
it is healthy, rather to be
living an unjudged rarity
such as enrichment
from the sight of your spectator
to forget that it remains wholly jealous subsides
stronger the crave of its rebellion
hunger-stupid has them all
who daren't ever go without
an agony in red
or a tragedy in black.

Of Principles and Precedents

If the worm
could fly,
the owls
and lots of other birds
would soon regret their love
for the earliest time.

Three Californians in Thailand

In accented fashion,
hair pushed up and prim,
primitive grins sliced their
material desires.
The Kodachrome casinos,
neon prisons with a tripod
of relations dressed in
bright-beige chinos,
chins up and in,
Rolex and Vostok
highlights in
brace-shackled wrists,
two halves of the same baht
paid, rolled, and gleams in tips
of the coin maiden,
and her flirtatious hips,
swaying around
pole-palaces and mosaic chalices;
ceramic and glass of their night,
one to slowly pass.

Ornate language,
one to recognise,
and street-spines
dressed in tuk-tuk drives,
hanging out of the
bookend-back seat;
the lingering sense of

dizzy hydration,
a nation of creation and inspiration.
Of beach towns to economic
disposal, the rage of
hysteria rinsed away
at the hostel.
Almost the time, in fact time never stops,
creeping reminders normality,
as if personas were developed
through this new era of humanity.

Asked the tending,
"What would it be?
A sparkling reflection,
I would owe it to pulsing times!
Or an erstwhile routine with hints
of lime?"
In oblivious chanting did
these modules of thrill celebrate,
their synchronised organisation,
and a gulp a tad late.
They hadn't left,
circled rumours on notes written by hand,
for they were only
three Californians in Thailand.

My Run Away Sleep

I am so sleepy
my hands are blue
shoved between a duvet, sheets, and pillows, two
the window is open
and the time is nine
I can hear the buzzing of a distant honey vine
the shadow walks into the room
and he shuts my door he crawls into my bed
and all night, he snores.

I am so sleepy
my belly is full
I finished my pleasure
like the lions near the bull
they growl and they hiss
like cut grass in the mist
the summer is sapphire
on the lakes of bliss
the clouds take their flight
like wings of birds and doves
flying in families
painting the sky pink and white above.

I am so sleepy
my soles are out
they are chilly
and they require warmth, this time about!
I'm not wearing socks
they are the wicked cover
they seem to adore the frost
on their cotton skin, the winter lover
but nipping goes
what footsteps are to the snow
the revenge of the treader
and the breeze on the toes
the song of my dreams
the night crosses fast, it seems.

I am so sleepy
my hair is drawn
like the hand of a painter
the dusk palette tints dawn
my hair in warmth
it glistens blonde, flaxen, yellow
whereas feeling shifts to blue
the mood carries mellow
the midnight drifts like a canoe in the sea
the lonesome traveller
on a horizon tsunami
he takes his oars like the eagle
and moves left, then tightly to the right
I am tight like the winds that he soars
in bed, the cocoon delight.

I am so sleepy
my eyes are low
the top of my curtains
are hung down the iris moons below
and the crack of twilight hinders my shutting;
through the refracting glass,
silhouettes of dust are blades to light's cutting
the crater disaster on a background of stars
messy and scrawled like the doodles of kids
the gleaming and glistening of lands too far
I am desperately in need to close my lids
everything is set in their special places
yet these thoughts are the only things my mind never erases.

I am so sleepy
it is nearly next three
the clock on the wall
he's angry at me
he reminded me almost six hours ago
the bed was the stage and
sleep was the show
I can't ignore to give my applause
to the hours, the days, and the years
but it was written in the ninth section of time's lowly clause
that six sections after I'd have signed away my fears
I cannot think about sleep even so
tiredness is the detriment to my lost slumber, I know.

I am so sleepy
the sky is getting bright
the summer air
it is cooler at night
it has me yearning for the imminent winter
a signal so strong like the thumb to a splinter

love is a lost hope in my hour of rest
it has me hoping for the days ahead
the common touch is a motion in jest
and reminds me I need to lay still, almost dead
for the tickle of rain that is soon to come
shone through the clouds on a stormy weather
it is shot from thunder, the heated lightning gun
and frightens me like nightmares to children
or words to ink feathers.

I am so sleepy
I cannot imagine
three jumping sheep
passing the gate near a cabin
the luscious green
is something I cannot see
skipping the valleys rinsed by timothy-tales on the nose, too
keen
and brooks are tipping, spilling with glee
the ball of heat is on the line
of ten lumps on an emerald spine
the rays stun the towns and the far away lands
while sinking in the quilt desert
are my weighted palm hands.

I am so sleepy
it is time to get up
but all I can think of
is the farmer's shepherd pup
the cutest little Bingo ever to be won
his eyes are as pretty as the rising sun
the flowers are blooming
and the herd, found in the gates
the ants are building cities that are moving
and the magpies are stealing silver watches
while cracking roof slates
the morning is the moment noise isn't found
only the owl dares to peep
I close my eyes, finally! I am, to myself, proud,
I can get to my run away sleep.

Virgins of Joy

Along we go
on the paths of crossing rumination
stood with harsh pain
it hurts to keep on this distant conversation
even if we are in the same room
our minds are gone, far from each other
you are not my friend
you are just a bother

so on I am alone
from distance to long times
we haven't seen these faces
nor have our steps since matched rhyme
a decade and another ten,
it has evenly divided us
some people grew in time, in size
we just grew cautious

and the days
the load it is a weight I cannot bear
my back gave in from resistance
and my legs, you kicked, you couldn't care
I tried to fight and crawl up, back
but lost whatever sense was left of sanity
we are virgins of joy
our love as fond as profanity.

Snow-Time Stranger and His Frosted Reason

This day my eyes opened
ten passing a startle typically felt instinct of alarm
it screamed
it screamed in a fashionably late charm
the window knew its gape
its 'sill-lip conversation
levitating with the friend, a curtain cape
enchanting room a fluttery glow
distant dawn's civilisation
the day, a third, in week beginning month
piles, folded the hills of snow
mounds shovelled freshly
frosted crest, breadth of ocean's
drift slow
the hanging sense of the season
I, a cold-cool stranger, locked in my frozen reason.

Waves of silver
dissipating bundles, crisp autumn, for winter it readily leaves
galloping freezing acres
the empty landscape carrying
storm-galleon thieves
purple depths
miles gone, dropped pebbles below under
trodden water, the hallowed deck
fond of the gallows
bitter nip of the quivering brow

swarming clouds atop grain flag
captured bolts, for now
the sense of the season
I, still a cool stranger, holding frozen reason.

The people are gathered
at the bus station
huddled around like igloo penguins
for breast-egg contemplation
the gust was blue
as was the wash, the spray of a yet-frozen puddle
the drivers, this morning,
seemed to have all their routes up-muddled
the children are waltzing on a nearby lake
as their lonesome mothers take their smoke breaks
like a community of impatient paper-people chains
they'll consider taking the day off
for they will not be doing this again
the coolest stranger am I this cheerful season
I stand here, I stand now, without a thawed reason.

After slipping on failed pavement cracks
I'm not yet paralysed
no, I'm just making my way back
my bed tempts me
like the duvet lady
she's a palm leaf shadow

I must admit, this chilly refuge is a tad shady
nonetheless, this is my single hour
the pillows missed me like Stanford power,
they are the guards
and I am the prisoner
I willingly keep my quilt shackles
as they play the institutionalised commissioners
they wrap me and inspect me,
am I worthy of such loving?
They test my answers
it is in this cavern I feel sheltered, I know only covering
the coolest stranger is sleepy this mellow season
he is lost with a sense of melted reason.

It has always been I and I alone
a king sits solitary
perched in the comfortable throne
I watch from the kingdom, I always have,
from a distance,
I hesitate to make first contact,
especially in this slippery instance
though, like the desperate calls of a walrus on ice,
may I meet my match in this idiot game, I must roll my dice,
for the company of anyone
platonic or true love
would feel slightly better
than to be independent, like a willing magpie
living in his cloud-land alone, above
I am the cool stranger
weightless in this festive season
though, now I see my nearest reason.

The years have gone
I am bitter this time
the sun has shone away his shine
and he creeps down the tinted horizon
even if it is midday
he longs for the veil, he yearns for the cover
of night's beautiful ways
if I am the sun,
there may, for me, be a moon,
stalking the galaxies, hoping
to find her perfect star soon
then, what am I doing?
Sitting in bed,
there are thousands more days
to dance away ahead
my moon, may the time marry us
the sparkle of winter bright
we shall waltz on many rivers
and skate through the cyan light
moon, we'll have our memories
hung on the wall
and the hazelnuts in a bowl, our bodies near the fire
this is our caricature of snow-time's fall
we are the coolest strangers of the season
and are frozen in our ways,
our similar reason.

Fair-Grounds

Fair-ground mystical,
migrate from tower
to city,
unjustified talent
of the crafting-man's
bomb,
implosion of thought
on the page of detonation,
debt-nation.

My Way on Lonely

Cashmere palace,
neon-stricken bending,
the psalm of
wedded kings;
commanding hand
to tune your
cello lungs
of exhale excellence.
One time more
to allow
my way on lonely.

One Our in a Day

The children
grew quiet.

I sat with you,
we listened
to the radio
of some collection
from decades ago.

You slept for
a tad-and-ten
while I counted my regrets
hopping
over fences and
clouds.

A tinnitus melody
and vertigo strums,
the aching verses
of my heart; I
desire the
our
of that day.

Statement of the Mind

True observation
should always be spoken;
whether in truth or passion,
and whether or not
the partnership ends broken,
or you fall out of fashion.

Neuroplasticity Incorporated

Blonde in palm readings
rent-out
born teething,
the grit of
perception,
where labels
are
conditioned,
where belief is taught real,
betrayed,
the ways they feel,
the concerning, discerning
the bankruptcy of needle-bound street living,
worth a few card-box shekels
and strips of gin-silver,
lay in the foamed
crest
of lip grieving.

A dendritic arborisation
of nylon elbows and powder
you worship the grain
of a heroine
who fought pain.
Depletion of the stem cell resin,
where gaps and tremors thrive,
addiction's foul stomach
lies in the incisors of guilt and

cries,
"Feed me,
hunger is alive
if only I tell you
sweet nothings and lies,
the hormone harlot
you are to the paving,
for a funeral
of ash cocaine,
and skull-malleable
dipped-saving!"
Weakened like
embryo
slaughtered at
embryo knife,
once in incision,
dead at the scythe,
the hassle of upbringing
and reuptake of
diffused emotion,
tampered the son
of Christ's willing temptation,
I carried you in
my basket of third revelations belated,
welcome to
Neuroplasticity Incorporated.

Spectacular! How rapid amazement directs only to disappointment

Lock and key, no? Knock, does he!
Have you heard the good news?
The resurrection of the angelic blessing,
how stunning to our now bountiful pleasures,
golden, sea-wrecked treasure,
locked, however, but we plead, listen!
We simply have a survey to offer, and
in time, you may receive;
in our guidance only you receive.

Cross our squares, no nightmares!
The question we ask next to you,
one of flavour, one so true.

What do the numbers of your arm
read?

And, as we,
yes, we,
and, as we,
yes, we,
wait so calmly, patiently!

Let us reassure you,
invite us indoors,
we will dust your ceiling
and rinse the floors!

And drive you up the wall
with our engine of illusion.

I am going to ask once more,
what is your number?

You are really efficient,
your prize, so near!
Oh, please, so kindly,
we are sensitive to fear!
And, as we wipe those joyful tears ...

I will be forced to prosecute you,
number Thirteen-One-Eighteen-Seven-One-Eighteen-Five-
Twenty.

The final question of this
questioning questionnaire,
happiness, happiness,
gratitude, gratitude,
emotions you'll soon wear!
Up next, the penultimate trial,
because we are chuckling at your
confusion, you have missed a line.

You crossed some numbers,
you've crossed a line.

Look at the line, take her to intensive
care. Leaking on the floor,
bleached clots everywhere.

Our inquiry,
your desired vehicle?
Stairs?
Whatever you say,
Thirteen-One-Eighteen-Seven-One-Eighteen-Five-Twenty!

Now we know you've anticipated this area of the survey, but
the important part is to stay conscious.
You will soon forget, for you will soon cease.
We would like you to report to us what you witness on our
one hundred percent, exclusive to survey-goers vitamin!

You shouldn't have invited us in, Margaret.
Is that Margaret gone now?

Fractured Petals

'Select the path to reach new tops,
canopies, mountain and glide,
distance from reality and
endurance-interrelated passion,
but in the avoidance of teaching
and befuddled escapism.'

The gold-faced stone read on illumination.
I fainted in the fragment of a lost second
like a now broken mandala clockwork
then danced through the
eternal deciphering of my
conceptions.

Is it so? In our lost time we find ourselves far?
Like the orange haze of a distant city
from the view of free-thought flight,
spinning in the turbulence of a flower firmament,
a heavenly plane strictly lacking
the understood conventions.
Is it so? In these distortions we are marooned, or
are we reinvented?

Cutting short, I must offer my advice.

Escape the seed that buries you,
it is a stressful purpose,
though hatching drives into preferential ventures,
long-term lectures to be washed out,
the irrelevance is stripped like cancer marrow,
so in favourable relevance and heightened adjudication,
part your mind from
your self-induced incubation.

Escape the seed, this mindful cage of metal
and blossom
in your uniquely and delicately fractured petals.

Cedar Rainfall

My face less glum
though not as much, shows no gum
nor grin to reveal my teeth, they aren't whitest
like the innocent glee of hooded juveniles
they are not as stained, each day I eat slightly less
there isn't interest on those that perceive
greatest commodity, no kind of best in jest
I'll be dead and damned in this perpetuity;
living this way, perhaps it is dying this way.

Boxes of stress, compartments of irritation
cubicle tantrum with the
reminders, many reminders
pinned on the cerebral walls
stems the postcard offers of stamped rejections
denial cavities that have stricken me low and dimly
lighting
future's pity length
by a spiteful April's evening attempts at lampposts
drowning in the ivy, the strays, and the cedar rainfall.

Hoax Woe

Oh, for the nemesis that calls
and calls and calls the conch hours
conscious echo in ripping tide's shallow shells
no lazy hermit in ruby etiquette dares
no earthworm slides the bitterness of a spiteful bay
the spirit of healing, monk-kissed the blessed sediments
extrapolating the secrets what treasures seem to have buried
there is no extraction from mining the graves
dead bodies of unreached gold, wrath of zombie indignation
dwells galleons sunken assured
whether it be the myth of their strength that has them capsized
or not
still raft-wise hypocrites raging in shanty sound.

Oh, for the rival that begs
and begs and begs the poorest hours
starved by defeatist method, unhinged by insufferable
what petty exchange, they desire in short copper debris
what I have to share of my time
our indefinite wallet, victimless where nobody takes it upon
themselves
to avoid the greatest thievery of age's unkind pension
no greater conviction than to be held accountable
our empty wallet, we tend to keep small memorabilia's
convention
in where the riches seem to hide, bad memory or the
nightmare
paid for by good intent
there is the enemy that strikes on short life
there is the rival that borderlines shorter sanity
kindness flawed like hoax, my fortune spun in the crops
makes leisure of those that tell real of humanity.

Sweetest Remedy Gone Sour

Hoping, though hopeless
the strung minds of poor form
trebled insurgency, years to the troubled emergency,
they cast a distasteful shadow
to each child made to bear another
born for birth and born again
twelve years, father and mother
extortion to the Neanderthal degree
should we learn? The obviously difficult
lesson of being free
or we'll give in
interrelation's generational excellency
otherwise truthfully, human simplicity

the tired games of ages ago
frequented by mass submission
schools tarnished by illiterate philosophy
challenged minds stretched like clay
to be hardened in cubicle atrocity
all the games that new children play
the struggle of withered finger
who tries to leader-point some more
children take that finger just to show them the door
grudge flows like sorrow rivers in and out, the bore
meanders like avoidance, makes oxbow of outcast
scars what has it insecure

graffiti is the rap of fine art
good lyric in messy execution
telling spirit in the walkie-talkie
as if intended to mask its absolution
there is perfection in the offhand
and that makes representation the start
following the command
of a good will's better heart
truth of soul wounds scrawled by felt-tip glory
in the underpass, splintered by squinting light's corridor story
advice delivered by lost storks
shamed by those too quick to the pitchfork
unchanging, the remedy of prone destruction
sour medicine on thinking tongues, sweet on obstruction.

Cold World Stressors

Uncertainty brings the shoreline out
coaxed into the modern world
multitude in this weird upbringing
perhaps turbulent goes of the abrasive way
temptation makes feeble of prior strong
wicked shades embarrassing
unlawful clouds make shambles of the sham
rain weariness over optimism
storms of drudgery
bleak and frightened and aching
dusty mannerism steals and taking
crumbs for the fat
as sacred dish of the lean
on any shoulder, there is brevity in this ego
takes hostage of attempted purity
dumbs over all that
pretends slyly, reveals too keen
broadway damnation, exalted woe
condemns the open arms to flawed security
cold world stressors, suppression of mortality realising
to trade a smile for angry brows, needless alligator
compromising.

April Eleventh Blues

I dreamed last night,
war on the television
to wake up on narrowed minds'
unwise superstition;
Volodymyr said it was genocide
Vladimir said nothing of the sort
cradled crazies take to hide
the modern glasses, papers contort

longer than the famous favela-man's fast
by five days, enrichment's incredulous excuse
feeling full is a thing of the past
prime-sinister as all-too loose
I dreamed last night,
war on the television
startled and distraught
as though this couldn't be
anything near real of a thought.

Escaping the seed is harder in strife …

About the Author

Ciaran Perks is an English poet and writer of the
'Illusory Poems' series. Growing up and living in Plymouth,
Devon, he has currently written three books, 'Peacocks',
'Moths', and 'Studies of Continuity'. At 19 years of age, he is set
to release many more poetry collections; continuing the
themes of life, dreams, and other illusory ideas.